Dare to Be SQUARE Afghans

Discover eight easy ways to make a big and beautiful square afghan! Each of these crochet designs from Lisa Gentry produces a captivating pattern of rich colors, with some resembling the artistry of patchwork quilts.

2

6

9

12

15

18

22

27

BONUS! **LOOK FOR THE CAMERA** in our instructions and watch our technique videos made just for you! **www.LeisureArts.com/6656**

LEISURE ARTS, INC. • Maumelle, Arkansas

Log Cabin

Finished Size: 55" (139.5 cm) square

EASY

SHOPPING LIST

Yarn (Medium Weight) 4 MEDIUM

[16 ounces, 812 yards

(454 grams, 742 meters) per skein**]**:

- ☐ Purple - 1 skein
- ☐ Lilac - 1 skein
- ☐ Rose - 1 skein
- ☐ Pink - 1 skein

Crochet Hook

- ☐ Size I (5.5 mm)

  or size needed for gauge

GAUGE INFORMATION

In pattern,

(ch 2, 3 dc) 3 times = 4" (10 cm);

6 rows = 3¾" (9.5 cm)

Gauge Swatch: 4½" (11.5 cm) square

Work same as Body through Row 6: 20 dc and 7 ch-2 sps.

INSTRUCTIONS

Body

With Purple, ch 6; join with slip st to form a ring.

Row 1: Ch 3 **(counts as first dc, now and throughout)**, (2 dc, ch 2, 3 dc) in ring: 6 dc and one ch-2 sp.

Row 2 (Right side)**:** Ch 5 **(counts as first dc plus ch 2, now and throughout)**, turn; (3 dc, ch 2) twice in next corner ch-2 sp, skip next 2 dc, dc in last dc: 8 dc and 3 ch-2 sps.

Note: Loop a short piece of yarn around any stitch to mark Row 2 as **right** side.

Row 3: Ch 3, turn; 2 dc in next ch-2 sp, ch 2, (3 dc, ch 2) twice in next corner ch-2 sp, 2 dc in next ch-2 sp, dc in last dc: 12 dc and 3 ch-2 sps.

Row 4: Ch 5, turn; 3 dc in next ch-2 sp, ch 2, (3 dc, ch 2) twice in next corner ch-2 sp, 3 dc in next ch-2 sp, ch 2, skip next 2 dc, dc in last dc: 14 dc and 5 ch-2 sps.

Row 5: Ch 3, turn; 2 dc in next ch-2 sp, ch 2, 3 dc in next ch-2 sp, ch 2, (3 dc, ch 2) twice in next corner ch-2 sp, 3 dc in next ch-2 sp, ch 2, 2 dc in next ch-2 sp, dc in last dc: 18 dc and 5 ch-2 sps.

Row 6: Ch 5, turn; (3 dc in next ch-2 sp, ch 2) twice, (3 dc, ch 2) twice in next corner ch-2 sp, (3 dc in next ch-2 sp, ch 2) twice, skip next 2 dc, dc in last dc changing to Lilac ***(Fig. A)***; cut Purple: 20 dc and 7 ch-2 sps.

Fig. A

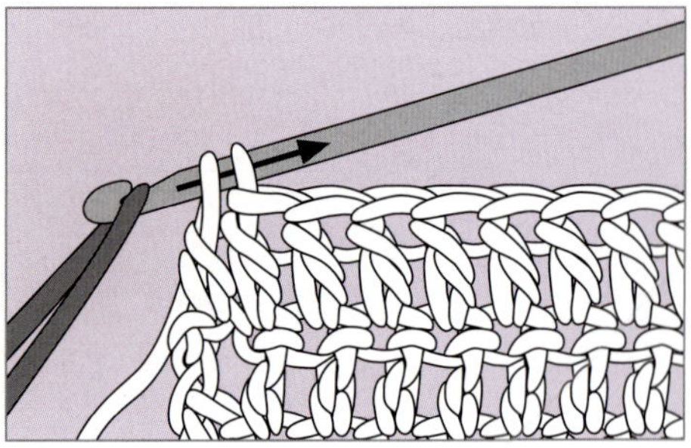

Row 7: Ch 3, turn; 2 dc in next ch-2 sp, ch 2, (3 dc in next ch-2 sp, ch 2) across to next corner ch-2 sp, (3 dc, ch 2) twice in corner ch-2 sp, (3 dc in next ch-2 sp, ch 2) across to last ch-2 sp, 2 dc in last ch-2 sp, dc in last dc: 24 dc and 7 ch-2 sps.

Row 8: Ch 5, turn; (3 dc in next ch-2 sp, ch 2) across to next corner ch-2 sp, (3 dc, ch 2) twice in corner ch-2 sp, (3 dc in next ch-2 sp, ch 2) across to last 3 dc, skip next 2 dc, dc in last dc: 26 dc and 9 ch-2 sps.

Rows 9-11: Repeat Rows 7 and 8 once, then repeat Row 7 once **more**: 36 dc and 11 ch-2 sps.

Row 12: Ch 5, turn; (3 dc in next ch-2 sp, ch 2) across to next corner ch-2 sp, (3 dc, ch 2) twice in corner ch-2 sp, (3 dc in next ch-2 sp, ch 2) across to last 3 dc, skip next 2 dc, dc in last dc changing to Pink; cut Lilac: 38 dc and 13 ch-2 sps.

Row 13: Ch 3, do **not** turn; working in ends of rows, 2 dc in first row, ch 2, (skip next row, 3 dc in next row, ch 2) 5 times, (3 dc, ch 2) twice in beginning ring, skip next row, (3 dc in next row, ch 2, skip next row) 5 times, 2 dc in last row, dc in top of last dc: 42 dc and 13 ch-2 sps.

Row 14: Ch 5, turn; (3 dc in next ch-2 sp, ch 2) across to next corner ch-2 sp, (3 dc, ch 2) twice in corner ch-2 sp, (3 dc in next ch-2 sp, ch 2) across to last 3 dc, skip next 2 dc, dc in last dc: 44 dc and 15 ch-2 sps.

Row 15: Ch 3, turn; 2 dc in next ch-2 sp, ch 2, (3 dc in next ch-2 sp, ch 2) across to next corner ch-2 sp, (3 dc, ch 2) twice in corner ch-2 sp, (3 dc in next ch-2 sp, ch 2) across to last ch-2 sp, 2 dc in last ch-2 sp, dc in last dc: 48 dc and 15 ch-2 sps.

Rows 16 and 17: Repeat Rows 14 and 15: 54 dc and 17 ch-2 sps.

Row 18: Ch 5, turn; (3 dc in next ch-2 sp, ch 2) across to next corner ch-2 sp, (3 dc, ch 2) twice in corner ch-2 sp, (3 dc in next ch-2 sp, ch 2) across to last 3 dc, skip next 2 dc, dc in last dc changing to Rose; cut Pink: 56 dc and 19 ch-2 sps.

Row 19: Ch 3, do **not** turn; working in ends of rows, 2 dc in first row, ch 2, skip next row, (3 dc in next row, ch 2, skip next row) twice, (3 dc in next ch-2 sp, ch 2) across to next corner ch-2 sp, (3 dc, ch 2) twice in corner ch-2 sp, (3 dc in next ch-2 sp, ch 2) across; working in ends of rows, skip first row, (3 dc in next row, ch 2, skip next row) twice, 2 dc in last row, dc in top of last dc: 60 dc and 19 ch-2 sps.

Rows 20-24: Repeat Rows 14-18, changing to Purple at end of Row 24; cut Rose: 74 dc and 25 ch-2 sps.

Row 25: Repeat Row 19: 78 dc and 25 ch-2 sps.

Rows 26-30: Repeat Rows 14-18, changing to Lilac at end of Row 30; cut Purple: 92 dc and 31 ch-2 sps.

Row 31: Repeat Row 19: 96 dc and 31 ch-2 sps.

Rows 32-36: Repeat Rows 14-18, changing to Pink at end of Row 36; cut Lilac: 110 dc and 37 ch-2 sps.

Row 37: Repeat Row 19: 114 dc and 37 ch-2 sps.

Rows 38-42: Repeat Rows 14-18, changing to Rose at end of Row 42; cut Pink: 128 dc and 43 ch-2 sps.

Row 43: Repeat Row 19: 132 dc and 43 ch-2 sps.

Rows 44-48: Repeat Rows 14-18; at end of Row 48, do **not** change colors: 146 dc and 49 ch-2 sps.

Row 49: Repeat Row 19: 150 dc and 49 ch-2 sps.

Rows 50-54: Repeat Rows 14-18, changing to Lilac at end of Row 54; cut Rose: 164 dc and 55 ch-2 sps.

Row 55: Repeat Row 19: 168 dc and 55 ch-2 sps.

Rows 56-60: Repeat Rows 14-18, changing to Pink at end of Row 60; cut Lilac: 182 dc and 61 ch-2 sps.

Row 61: Repeat Row 19: 186 dc and 61 ch-2 sps.

Rows 62-66: Repeat Rows 14-18, changing to Purple at end of Row 66; cut Pink: 200 dc and 67 ch-2 sps.

Row 67: Repeat Row 19: 204 dc and 67 ch-2 sps.

Rows 68-72: Repeat Rows 14-18, changing to Rose at end of Row 72; cut Purple: 218 dc and 73 ch-2 sps.

Row 73: Repeat Row 19: 222 dc and 73 ch-2 sps.

Rows 74-78: Repeat Rows 14-18, changing to Lilac at end of Row 78; cut Rose: 236 dc and 79 ch-2 sps.

Row 79: Repeat Row 19: 240 dc and 79 ch-2 sps.

Rows 80-84: Repeat Rows 14-18, changing to Pink at end of Row 84; cut Lilac: 254 dc and 85 ch-2 sps.

Row 85: Repeat Row 19: 258 dc and 85 ch-2 sps.

Rows 86-90: Repeat Rows 14-18, changing to Purple at end of Row 90; cut Pink: 272 dc and 91 ch-2 sps.

Trim: Ch 5, turn; 3 dc in first ch-2 sp, † 5 dc in each ch-2 sp across to next corner ch-2 sp, (3 dc, ch 2, 3 dc) in corner ch-2 sp †, 5 dc in each of next 44 ch-2 sps, (3 dc, ch 2, 3 dc) in last sp; working in ends of rows, skip next row, (5 dc in next row, skip next row) twice, repeat from † to † once, 5 dc in each of next 42 ch-2 sps; working in ends of rows, skip next row, (5 dc in next row, skip next row) twice, 2 dc in last row; join with slip st to first dc, finish off.

Earthy Shadows

Finished Size: 56" (142 cm) square

EASY

SHOPPING LIST

Yarn (Medium Weight) MEDIUM 4

[3.5 ounces, 208 yards (100 grams, 190 meters) per skein]:

- ☐ Tan - 7 skeins
- ☐ Variegated - 5 skeins

Crochet Hook

- ☐ Size I (5.5 mm) **or** size needed for gauge

GAUGE INFORMATION

In pattern,

[sc, ch 1, (tr, ch 1) 5 times] twice and Rnds 1-4 = 5" (12.75 cm)

Gauge Swatch: 5" (12.75 cm) square

Work same as Body through Rnd 4: 24 tr, 8 Clusters, and 16 sps.

STITCH GUIDE

TREBLE CROCHET ***(abbreviated tr)***

YO twice, insert hook in sp indicated, YO and pull up a loop (4 loops on hook), (YO and draw through 2 loops on hook) 3 times.

CLUSTER (uses one ch-1 sp)

★ YO twice, insert hook in ch-1 sp indicated, YO and pull up a loop, (YO and draw through 2 loops on hook) twice; repeat from ★ 2 times **more**, YO and draw through all 4 loops on hook.

INSTRUCTIONS

Body

With Variegated, ch 6; join with slip st to form a ring.

Rnd 1 (Right side)**:** Ch 5 **(counts as first dc plus ch 2)**, (dc in ring, ch 2) 7 times; join with slip st to first dc, finish off: 8 dc and 8 ch-2 sps.

Note: Loop a short piece of yarn around any stitch to mark Rnd 1 as **right** side.

Rnd 2: With **right** side facing, join Tan with dc in any ch-2 sp ***(see Joining With Dc, page 31)***; dc in same sp, ch 2, (2 dc in next ch-2 sp, ch 2) around; join with slip st to first dc, finish off: 16 dc and 8 ch-2 sps.

Rnd 3: With **right** side facing, join Variegated with sc in any ch-2 sp ***(see Joining With Sc, page 31)***; ch 1, (dc, ch 1) 5 times in next ch-2 sp, ★ sc in next ch-2 sp, ch 1, (dc, ch 1) 5 times in next ch-2 sp; repeat from ★ 2 times **more**; join with slip st to first sc, finish off: 24 sts and 24 ch-1 sps.

Rnd 4: With **right** side facing, join Tan with slip st in ch-1 sp **before** center dc of any 5-dc group; ch 4 **(counts as first tr, now and throughout)**, 2 tr in same sp, ch 3, 3 tr in next ch-1 sp, ch 3, ★ † work Cluster in next ch-1 sp, ch 1, skip next 2 ch-1 sps, work Cluster in next ch-1 sp, ch 3 †, (3 tr in next ch-1 sp, ch 3) twice; repeat from ★ 2 times **more**, then repeat from † to † once; join with slip st to first tr, finish off: 32 sts and 16 sps.

VIRGINIA
PRIVATE DREAM
OF PUBLIC PEOP

Rnd 5: With **right** side facing, join Variegated with slip st in any corner ch-3 sp; ch 4, (2 tr, ch 3, 3 tr) in same sp, ★ † ch 1, (dc, ch 1) 5 times in next ch-3 sp, sc in next ch-1 sp, ch 1, (dc, ch 1) 5 times in next ch-3 sp †, (3 tr, ch 3, 3 tr) in next corner ch-3 sp; repeat from ★ 2 times **more**, then repeat from † to † once; join with slip st to first tr, finish off: 68 sts and 52 sps.

Rnd 6: With **right** side facing, join Tan with slip st in any corner ch-3 sp; ch 4, (2 tr, ch 3, 3 tr) in same sp, ★ † ch 1, skip next ch-1 sp, work Cluster in next ch-1 sp, ch 3, sc in next ch-1 sp, ch 1, sc in next ch-1 sp, ch 3, work Cluster in next ch-1 sp, ch 1, skip next 2 ch-1 sps, work Cluster in next ch-1 sp, ch 3, sc in next ch-1 sp, ch 1, sc in next ch-1 sp, ch 3, work Cluster in next ch-1 sp, ch 1 †, (3 tr, ch 3, 3 tr) in next corner ch-3 sp; repeat from ★ 2 times **more**, then repeat from † to † once; join with slip st to first tr, finish off: 56 sts and 40 sps.

Rnd 7: With **right** side facing, join Variegated with slip st in any corner ch-3 sp; ch 4, (2 tr, ch 3, 3 tr) in same sp, ★ † ch 1, (dc, ch 1) 5 times in next ch-1 sp, **[**skip next ch-3 sp, sc in next ch-1 sp, ch 1, skip next ch-3 sp, (dc, ch 1) 5 times in next ch-1 sp**]** twice †, (3 tr, ch 3, 3 tr) in corner ch-3 sp; repeat from ★ 2 times **more**, then repeat from † to † once; join with slip st to first tr, finish off: 92 sts and 76 sps.

Rnd 8: With **right** side facing, join Tan with slip st in any corner ch-3 sp; ch 4, (2 tr, ch 3, 3 tr) in same sp, ★ † ch 1, skip next ch-1 sp, work Cluster in next ch-1 sp, ch 3, sc in next ch-1 sp, ch 1, sc in next ch-1 sp, ch 3, work Cluster in next ch-1 sp, ch 1, **[**skip next 2 ch-1 sps, work Cluster in next ch-1 sp, ch 3, sc in next ch-1 sp, ch 1, sc in next ch-1 sp, ch 3, work Cluster in next ch-1 sp, ch 1**]** across to next corner ch-3 sp †, (3 tr, ch 3, 3 tr) in corner ch-3 sp; repeat from ★ 2 times **more**, then repeat from † to † once; join with slip st to first tr, finish off: 72 sts and 56 sps.

Rnd 9: With **right** side facing, join Variegated with slip st in any corner ch-3 sp; ch 4, (2 tr, ch 3, 3 tr) in same sp, ★ † ch 1, (dc, ch 1) 5 times in next ch-1 sp, **[**skip next ch-3 sp, sc in next ch-1 sp, ch 1, skip next ch-3 sp, (dc, ch 1) 5 times in next ch-1 sp**]** across to next corner ch-3 sp †, (3 tr, ch 3, 3 tr) in corner ch-3 sp; repeat from ★ 2 times **more**, then repeat from † to † once; join with slip st to first tr, finish off: 116 sts and 100 sps.

Rnds 10-40: Repeat Rnds 8 and 9, 15 times; then repeat Rnd 8 once **more**: 328 sts and 312 sps.

Rnd 41: With **right** side facing, join Variegated with slip st in any corner ch-3 sp, ch 4, (2 tr, ch 3, 3 tr) in same sp, ★ † ch 1, (tr, ch 1) 6 times in next ch-1 sp, **[**skip next ch-3 sp, sc in next ch-1 sp, ch 1, skip next ch-3 sp, (tr, ch 1) 6 times in next ch-1 sp**]** across to next corner ch-3 sp †, (3 tr, ch 3, 3 tr) in corner ch-3 sp; repeat from ★ 2 times **more**, then repeat from † to † once; join with slip st to first tr, finish off: 580 sts and 564 sps.

Rnd 42: With **right** side facing, join Tan with slip st in any corner ch-3 sp; ch 4, 6 tr in same sp, ★ † ch 2, skip next 2 tr, sc in next tr, skip next ch-1 sp, **[**(2 dc in next ch-1 sp, ch 1) twice, (2 dc, ch 1) twice in next ch-1 sp, 2 dc in next ch-1 sp, ch 1, 2 dc in next ch-1 sp, skip next ch-1 sp, sc in next st**]** across to within 2 tr of next corner ch-3 sp, ch 2, skip next 2 tr †, 7 tr in corner ch-3 sp; repeat from ★ 2 times **more**, then repeat from † to † once; join with slip st to first tr, finish off.

Jewels

Shown on page 11.

Finished Size: 57" (145 cm) square

EASY

SHOPPING LIST

Yarn (Medium Weight) MEDIUM 4

[5 ounces, 256 yards

(141 grams, 234 meters) per skein]:

- ☐ Wine - 4 skeins
- ☐ Gold - 4 skeins
- ☐ Blue - 4 skeins
- ☐ Green - 3 skeins

Crochet Hook

- ☐ Size K (6.5 mm)

  or size needed for gauge

GAUGE INFORMATION

In pattern,

2 stitch repeats = 3¼" (8.25 cm) wide

Rnds 1-5 = 5" (12.75 cm)

Gauge Swatch: 5" (12.75 cm) square

Work same as Body through Rnd 5: 40 dc and 24 sps.

STITCH GUIDE

TREBLE CROCHET *(abbreviated tr)*

YO twice, insert hook in sp indicated, YO and pull up a loop (4 loops on hook), (YO and draw through 2 loops on hook) 3 times.

COLOR SEQUENCE

2 Rnds **each:** ★ (Blue, Wine) twice, Gold, Green, Gold; repeat from ★ 2 times **more**, Blue, Wine, Gold, Green, Blue, Wine, Gold.

INSTRUCTIONS

Body

With Blue, ch 6; join with slip st to form a ring.

Rnd 1 (Right side)**:** Ch 5, (dc, ch 2) 7 times in ring; join with slip st to third ch of beginning ch-5: 8 sts and 8 ch-2 sps.

Note: Loop a short piece of yarn around any stitch to mark Rnd 1 as **right** side.

Rnd 2: Slip st in next ch-2 sp, ch 3 **(counts as first dc, now and throughout)**, dc in same sp, ch 2, (2 dc in next ch-2 sp, ch 2) around; join with slip st to first dc: 16 dc and 8 ch-2 sps.

Rnd 3: Slip st in next dc and in next ch-2 sp, ch 4, dc in same sp, ch 1, (2 dc, ch 4, 2 dc) in next ch-2 sp, ch 1, ★ (dc, ch 1) twice in next ch-2 sp, (2 dc, ch 4, 2 dc) in next ch-2 sp, ch 1; repeat from ★ 2 times **more**; join with slip st to third ch of beginning ch-4, finish off: 24 sts and 16 sps.

Rnd 4: With **right** side facing, join Wine with slip st in any corner ch-4 sp; ch 7 **(counts as first dc plus ch 4, now and throughout)**, dc in same sp, ★ † ch 1, working **around** next ch *(Fig. 1, page 31)*, (tr, ch 1) twice in corner ch-2 sp on Rnd 2 (after last corner dc), skip next dc, sc in next ch-1 sp, ch 1, working **around** next ch, (tr, ch 1) twice in corner ch-2 sp on Rnd 2 (before first corner dc) †, (dc, ch 4, dc) in next corner ch-4 sp; repeat from ★ 2 times **more**, then repeat from † to † once; join with slip st to first dc: 28 sts and 28 sps.

Rnd 5: (Slip st, ch 7, dc) in next corner ch-4 sp, ★ † ch 1, skip next ch-1 sp, (2 dc, ch 1) twice in next ch-1 sp, skip next 2 ch-1 sps, (2 dc, ch 1) twice in next ch-1 sp, skip next ch-1 sp †, (dc, ch 4, dc) in next corner ch-4 sp; repeat from ★ 2 times **more**, then repeat from † to † once; join with slip st to first dc, finish off: 40 dc and 24 sps.

Rnd 6: With **right** side facing, join Gold with slip st in any corner ch-4 sp; ch 7, dc in same sp, ★ † ch 1, working **around** last 2 rnds, (tr, ch 1) twice in corner ch-4 sp on Rnd 3, sc in next ch-1 sp, ch 1, working **around** last 2 rnds, (tr, ch 1) twice in ch-1 sp on Rnd 3 (same sp as sc), sc in next ch-1 sp, ch 1, working **around** last 2 rnds, (tr, ch 1) twice in corner ch-4 sp on Rnd 3 †, (dc, ch 4, dc) in next corner ch-4 sp; repeat from ★ 2 times **more**, then repeat from † to † once; join with slip st to first dc: 40 sts and 40 sps.

Rnd 7: (Slip st, ch 7, dc) in next corner ch-4 sp, ★ † ch 1, skip next ch-1 sp, (2 dc, ch 1) twice in next ch-1 sp, [skip next 2 ch-1 sps, (2 dc, ch 1) twice in next ch-1 sp] twice, skip next ch-1 sp †, (dc, ch 4, dc) in next corner ch-4 sp; repeat from ★ 2 times **more**, then repeat from † to † once; join with slip st to first dc, finish off: 56 dc and 32 sps.

Rnd 8: With **right** side facing, join Green with slip st in any corner ch-4 sp; ch 7, dc in same sp, ★ † ch 1, working **around** last 2 rnds, (tr, ch 1) twice in corner ch-4 sp **below**, sc in next ch-1 sp, ch 1, [working **around** last 2 rnds, (tr, ch 1) twice in ch-1 sp **below**, sc in next ch-1 sp, ch 1] across to within one ch-1 sp of next corner ch-4 sp, working **around** last 2 rnds, (tr, ch 1) twice in corner ch-4 sp **below** †, (dc, ch 4, dc) in next corner ch-4 sp; repeat from ★ 2 times **more**, then repeat from † to † once; join with slip st to first dc: 52 sts and 52 sps.

Rnd 9: (Slip st, ch 7, dc) in next corner ch-4 sp, ★ † ch 1, skip next ch-1 sp, (2 dc, ch 1) twice in next ch-1 sp, [skip next 2 ch-1 sps, (2 dc, ch 1) twice in next ch-1 sp] across to within one ch-1 sp of next corner ch-4 sp, skip next ch-1 sp †, (dc, ch 4, dc) in next corner ch-4 sp; repeat from ★ 2 times **more**, then repeat from † to † once; join with slip st to first dc, finish off: 72 dc and 40 sps.

Rnds 10-65: Following Color Sequence, repeat Rnds 8 and 9, 28 times: 520 dc and 264 sps.

Rnd 66: With **right** side facing, join Green with slip st in any corner ch-4 sp; ch 3, (2 dc, ch 2, 3 dc) in same sp, ★ † ch 1, working **around** last 2 rnds, (tr, ch 1) twice in corner ch-4 sp **below**, sc in next ch-1 sp, ch 1, [working **around** last 2 rnds, (tr, ch 1) twice in ch-1 sp **below**, sc in next ch-1 sp, ch 1] across to within one ch-1 sp of next corner ch-4 sp, working **around** last 2 rnds, (tr, ch 1) twice in corner ch-4 sp **below** †, (3 dc, ch 2, 3 dc) in next corner ch-4 sp; repeat from ★ 2 times **more**, then repeat from † to † once; join with slip st to first dc: 416 sts and 400 sps.

Rnd 67: Slip st in next 2 dc and in next ch-2 sp, ch 3, (3 dc, ch 1, 4 dc) in same sp, ch 1, ★ † skip next ch-1 sp, (dc, 3 tr, dc) in next ch-1 sp, ch 1, skip next ch-1 sp, [sc in next sc, ch 1, skip next ch-1 sp, (dc, 3 tr, dc) in next ch-1 sp, ch 1, skip next ch-1 sp] across to next corner ch-2 sp †, (4 dc, ch 1) twice in corner ch-2 sp; repeat from ★ 2 times **more**, then repeat from † to † once; join with slip st to first dc, finish off.

Patchwork

Finished Size: 55" (139.5 cm) square

EASY

SHOPPING LIST

Yarn (Medium Weight) 4

[4 ounces, 200 yards
(113 grams, 183 meters) per skein]:

- ☐ Tan - 7 skeins
- ☐ Green - 6 skeins

Crochet Hook

- ☐ Size J (6 mm)
  or size needed for gauge

GAUGE INFORMATION

In pattern,
slip st, ch 1, (dtr, ch 1) 5 times = 3" (7.5 cm)
4 rnds =3¼" (8.25 cm)

Gauge Swatch: 6" (15.25 cm) square
Work same as Body through Rnd 4: 8 Clusters.

STITCH GUIDE

TREBLE CROCHET

(abbreviated tr)

YO twice, insert hook in sp indicated, YO and pull up a loop (4 loops on hook), (YO and draw through 2 loops on hook) 3 times.

DOUBLE TREBLE CROCHET

(abbreviated dtr)

YO 3 times, insert hook in st indicated, YO and pull up a loop (5 loops on hook), (YO and draw through 2 loops on hook) 4 times.

3-DTR CLUSTER

(uses next 3 ch-1 sps)

★ YO 3 times, insert hook in **next** ch-1 sp, YO and pull up a loop, (YO and draw through 2 loops on hook) 3 times; repeat from ★ 2 times **more**, YO and draw through all 4 loops on hook, ch 1 to close.

6-DTR CLUSTER

(uses next 6 ch-1 sps)

★ YO 3 times, insert hook in **next** ch-1 sp, YO and pull up a loop, (YO and draw through 2 loops on hook) 3 times; repeat from ★ 5 times **more**, YO and draw through all 7 loops on hook, ch 1 to close.

INSTRUCTIONS

Body

With Tan, ch 5; join with slip st to form a ring.

Rnd 1 (Right side): Ch 5 **(counts as first tr plus ch 1)**, (tr, ch 1) 11 times in ring; join with slip st to first tr, finish off: 12 ch-1 sps.

Note: Loop a short piece of yarn around any stitch to mark Rnd 1 as **right** side.

Rnd 2: With **right** side facing, join Green with slip st in any tr; ch 5, work 3-dtr Cluster, ch 5, ★ slip st in next tr, ch 5, work 3-dtr Cluster, ch 5; repeat from ★ 2 times **more**; join with slip st to first slip st: 4 3-dtr Clusters.

Rnd 3: Ch 1, (dtr, ch 1) 8 times in next 3-dtr Cluster (closing ch), ★ slip st in next slip st, ch 1, (dtr, ch 1) 8 times in next 3-dtr Cluster; repeat from ★ 2 times **more**; join with slip st to joining slip st, finish off: 32 dtr and 36 ch-1 sps.

Rnd 4: With **right** side facing, join Tan with slip st in third dtr of any corner 8-dtr group; ★ † ch 5, work 3-dtr Cluster, ch 5, slip st in next dtr, ch 5, work 6-dtr Cluster, ch 5 †, slip st in next dtr; repeat from ★ 2 times **more**, then repeat from † to † once; join with slip st to joining slip st: 8 Clusters.

Rnd 5: ★ † Ch 1, (dtr, ch 1) 8 times in next 3-dtr Cluster, slip st in next slip st, ch 1, (dtr, ch 1) 5 times in next 6-dtr Cluster (closing ch) †, slip st in next slip st; repeat from ★ 2 times **more**, then repeat from † to † once; join with slip st to joining slip st, finish off: 52 dtr and 60 ch-1 sps.

Rnd 6: With **right** side facing, join Green with slip st in third dtr of any corner 8-dtr group; ★ † ch 5, work 3-dtr Cluster, ch 5, [slip st in next dtr, ch 5, work 6-dtr Cluster, ch 5] across to next corner †, slip st in next dtr; repeat from ★ 2 times **more**, then repeat from † to † once; join with slip st to joining slip st: 12 Clusters.

Rnd 7: ★ † Ch 1, (dtr, ch 1) 8 times in next corner 3-dtr Cluster, [slip st in next slip st, ch 1, (dtr, ch 1) 5 times in next 6-dtr Cluster] across to within one slip st of next corner 3-dtr Cluster †, slip st in next slip st; repeat from ★ 2 times **more**, then repeat from † to † once; join with slip st to joining slip st, finish off: 72 dtr and 84 ch-1 sps.

Rnd 8: With **right** side facing, join Tan with slip st in third dtr of any corner 8-dtr group; ★ † ch 5, work 3-dtr Cluster, ch 5, [slip st in next dtr, ch 5, work 6-dtr Cluster, ch 5] across to next corner †, slip st in next dtr; repeat from ★ 2 times **more**, then repeat from † to † once; join with slip st to joining slip st: 16 Clusters.

Rnd 9: ★ † Ch 1, (dtr, ch 1) 8 times in next corner 3-dtr Cluster, [slip st in next slip st, ch 1, (dtr, ch 1) 5 times in next 6-dtr Cluster] across to within one slip st of next corner 3-dtr Cluster †, slip st in next slip st; repeat from ★ 2 times **more**, then repeat from † to † once; join with slip st to joining slip st, finish off: 92 dtr and 108 ch-1 sps.

Rnds 10-32: Repeat Rnds 6-9, 5 times; then repeat Rnds 6-8 once **more**: 64 Clusters.

Rnd 33: Ch 4, slip st in same st as joining, ★ † ch 2, dtr in next corner 3-dtr Cluster, (ch 1, dtr in same st) 8 times, ch 2, [(slip st, ch 4, slip st) in next slip st, ch 2, dtr in next 6-dtr Cluster, (ch 1, dtr in same st) 5 times, ch 2] across to within one slip st of next corner 3-dtr Cluster †, (slip st, ch 4, slip st) in next slip st; repeat from ★ 2 times **more**, then repeat from † to † once; join with slip st to joining slip st, finish off.

Patriotic Lace

Shown on page 17.

Finished Size: 51½" (131.5 cm) square

EASY

SHOPPING LIST

Yarn (Medium Weight) MEDIUM 4
[6 ounces, 315 yards
(170.1 grams, 288 meters)
per skein]:

- ☐ Off White - 3 skeins
- ☐ Blue - 3 skeins
- ☐ Red - 3 skeins

Crochet Hook

- ☐ Size I (5.5 mm)
  or size needed for gauge

GAUGE INFORMATION

In pattern,
[sc, ch 1, (dc, ch 1) 6 times] twice
= 4¾" (12 cm);
Rnds 1-7 = 8" (20.25 cm)

Gauge Swatch: 8" (20.25 cm) square
Work same as Body through Rnd 7:
84 sts and 68 sps.

INSTRUCTIONS

Body

With Off White, ch 5; join with slip st to form a ring.

Rnd 1 (Right side)**:** Ch 4 **(counts as first dc plus ch 1, now and throughout)**, dc in ring, ch 3, (dc, ch 1, dc, ch 3) 3 times in ring; join with slip st to first dc: 8 dc and 8 sps.

Note: Loop a short piece of yarn around any stitch to mark Rnd 1 as **right** side.

Rnd 2: Slip st in next ch-1 sp, ch 3 **(counts as first dc, now and throughout)**, 2 dc in same sp, ch 1, (2 dc, ch 3, 2 dc) in next ch-3 sp, ch 1, ★ 3 dc in next ch-1 sp, ch 1, (2 dc, ch 3, 2 dc) in next ch-3 sp, ch 1; repeat from ★ 2 times **more**; join with slip st to first dc, finish off: 28 dc and 12 sps.

Rnd 3: With **right** side facing, join Blue with dc in any corner ch-3 sp ***(see Joining With Dc, page 31)***; (dc, ch 3, 2 dc) in same sp, ★ † ch 3, sc in next ch-1 sp, ch 4, sc in next ch-1 sp, ch 3 †, (2 dc, ch 3, 2 dc) in next corner ch-3 sp; repeat from ★ 2 times **more**, then repeat from † to † once; join with slip st to first dc: 24 sts and 16 sps.

Rnd 4: Slip st in next dc and in next corner ch-3 sp, ch 3, (2 dc, ch 4, 3 dc) in same sp, ★ † ch 1, skip next ch-3 sp, (dc, ch 1) 6 times in next ch-4 sp, skip next ch-3 sp †, (3 dc, ch 4, 3 dc) in next corner ch-3 sp; repeat from ★ 2 times **more**, then repeat from † to † once; join with slip st to first dc, finish off: 48 dc and 32 sps.

Rnd 5: With **right** side facing, join Red with dc in any corner ch-4 sp; (dc, ch 3, 2 dc) in same sp, ★ † ch 1, dc in next 3 dc and in next 3 ch-1 sps, ch 2, sc in next ch-1 sp, ch 2, dc in next 3 ch-1 sps and in next 3 dc, ch 1 †, (2 dc, ch 3, 2 dc) in next corner ch-4 sp; repeat from ★ 2 times **more**, then repeat from † to † once; join with slip st to first dc: 68 sts and 20 sps.

Rnd 6: Slip st in next dc and in next corner ch-3 sp; ch 3, (dc, ch 3, 2 dc) in same sp, ★ † ch 1, dc in next dc, ch 3, skip next dc, sc in next dc, ch 4, skip next 4 dc, sc in next dc, ch 3, dc in next sc, ch 3, sc in next dc, ch 4, skip next 4 dc, sc in next dc, ch 3, skip next dc, dc in next dc, ch 1 †, (2 dc, ch 3, 2 dc) in next corner ch-3 sp; repeat from ★ 2 times **more**, then repeat from † to † once; join with slip st to first dc: 44 sts and 36 sps.

Rnd 7: Slip st in next dc and in next corner ch-3 sp; ch 3, (2 dc, ch 4, 3 dc) in same sp, ★ † ch 1, skip next 2 dc, sc in next dc, ch 1, [skip next ch-3 sp, (dc, ch 1) 6 times in next ch-4 sp, skip next ch-3 sp, sc in next dc, ch 1] twice, skip next ch-1 sp †, (3 dc, ch 4, 3 dc) in next corner ch-4 sp; repeat from ★ 2 times **more**, then repeat from † to † once; join with slip st to first dc, finish off: 84 sts and 68 sps.

Rnd 8: With **right** side facing, join Off White with dc in any corner ch-4 sp; (dc, ch 3, 2 dc) in same sp, ★ † ch 1, skip next dc, dc in next 2 dc and in next ch-1 sp, skip next sc, [dc in next 3 ch-1 sps, ch 2, sc in next ch-1 sp, ch 2, dc in next 3 ch-1 sps, skip next sc] across to within one ch-1 sp of next corner ch-4 sp, dc in next ch-1 sp and in next 2 dc, ch 1 †, (2 dc, ch 3, 2 dc) in corner ch-4 sp; repeat from ★ 2 times **more**, then repeat from † to † once; join with slip st to first dc: 96 sts and 28 sps.

Rnd 9: Slip st in next dc and in next corner ch-3 sp; ch 3, (dc, ch 3, 2 dc) in same sp, ★ † ch 1, skip next dc, dc in next dc, ch 3, sc in next dc, ch 4, skip next 4 dc, sc in next dc, ch 3, [dc in next sc, ch 3, sc in next dc, ch 4, skip next 4 dc, sc in next dc, ch 3] across to within one ch-1 sp of next corner ch-3 sp, skip next ch-1 sp, dc in next dc, ch 1 †, (2 dc, ch 3, 2 dc) in corner ch-3 sp; repeat from ★ 2 times **more**, then repeat from † to † once; join with slip st to first dc: 56 sts and 48 sps.

Rnd 10: Slip st in next dc and in next corner ch-3 sp, ch 3, (2 dc, ch 4, 3 dc) in same sp, ★ † ch 1, skip next 2 dc, sc in next dc, ch 1, [skip next ch-3 sp, (dc, ch 1) 6 times in next ch-4 sp, skip next ch-3 sp, sc in next dc, ch 1] across to within one ch-1 sp of next corner ch-3 sp, skip next ch-1 sp †, (3 dc, ch 4, 3 dc) in corner ch-3 sp; repeat from ★ 2 times **more**, then repeat from † to † once; join with slip st to first dc, finish off: 112 sts and 96 sps.

Rnds 11-13: With Blue, repeat Rnds 8-10: 140 sts and 124 sps.

Rnds 14-16: With Red, repeat Rnds 8-10: 168 sts and 152 sps.

Rnds 17-57: Repeat Rnds 8-16, 4 times; then repeat Rnds 8-12 once **more**: 248 sts and 240 sps.

Rnd 58: Slip st in next dc and in next corner ch-3 sp, ch 4, dc in same sp, (ch 1, dc in same sp) 7 times, ★ † ch 2, skip next 2 dc, sc in next dc, ch 2, [skip next ch-3 sp, dc in next ch-4 sp, (ch 1, dc in same sp) 5 times, ch 2, skip next ch-3 sp, sc in next dc, ch 2] across to within one ch-1 sp of next corner ch-3 sp, skip next ch-1 sp †, dc in corner ch-3 sp, (ch 1, dc in same sp) 8 times; repeat from ★ 2 times **more**, then repeat from † to † once; join with slip st to first dc, finish off.

PRINCE HALVERSON
Underside of Joy
FRANK'S
forever young

Pink Passion

Finished Size: 51" (129.5 cm) square

EASY

SHOPPING LIST

Yarn (Medium Weight) 4

[3.5 ounces, 170 yards
(100 grams, 156 meters) per skein]:

- ☐ Pink - 4 skeins
- ☐ Dk Pink - 4 skeins
- ☐ Brown - 4 skeins

Crochet Hook

- ☐ Size K (6.5 mm)
  or size needed for gauge

GAUGE INFORMATION

In pattern,
(dc, ch 1) 5 times and 3 sc = 3" (7.5 cm)
Rnds 1-6 = 7" (17.75 cm)

Gauge Swatch: 7" (17.75 cm) square
Work same as Body through Rnd 6: 32 sts and 16 sps.

STITCH GUIDE

CLUSTER

(uses 4 ch-1 sps and one sc)

† YO, insert hook in **next** ch-1 sp, YO and pull up a loop, YO and draw through 2 loops on hook †; repeat from † to † once **more**, YO, skip next sc, insert hook in next sc, YO and pull up a loop, YO and draw through 2 loops on hook, repeat from † to † twice, YO and draw through all 6 loops on hook, ch 1 to close.

INSTRUCTIONS

Body

With Pink, ch 6; join with slip st to form a ring.

Rnd 1 (Right side): Ch 3 **(counts as first dc, now and throughout)**, 3 dc in ring, ch 2, (4 dc in ring, ch 2) 3 times; join with slip st to first dc, finish off: 16 dc and 4 ch-2 sps.

Note: Loop a short piece of yarn around any stitch to mark Rnd 1 as **right** side.

Rnd 2: With **right** side facing, join Dk Pink with slip st in any ch-2 sp; ch 3, (dc, ch 2, 2 dc) in same sp, ch 1, skip next dc, (sc in next dc, ch 1) twice, ★ (2 dc, ch 2, 2 dc) in next ch-2 sp, ch 1, skip next dc, (sc in next dc, ch 1) twice; repeat from ★ 2 times **more**; join with slip st to first dc: 24 sts and 16 sps.

Rnd 3: Slip st in next dc and in next ch-2 sp, ch 4 **(counts as first dc plus ch 1, now and throughout)**, (dc in same sp, ch 1) 4 times, skip next ch-1 sp, sc in next sc, sc in next ch-1 sp and in next sc, ch 1, skip next ch-1 sp, ★ (dc, ch 1) 5 times in next ch-2 sp, skip next ch-1 sp, sc in next sc, sc in next ch-1 sp and in next sc, ch 1, skip next ch-1 sp; repeat from ★ 2 times **more**; join with slip st to first dc, finish off: 32 sts and 24 ch-1 sps.

Rnd 4: With **right** side facing, join Brown with sc in ch-1 sp **after** center dc of any corner 5-dc group *(see Joining With Sc, page 31)*; 2 sc in same sp, ch 4, work Cluster, ch 4, 3 sc in next ch-1 sp, ch 3, ★ 3 sc in next ch-1 sp, ch 4, work Cluster, ch 4, 3 sc in next ch-1 sp, ch 3; repeat from ★ 2 times **more**; join with slip to first sc: 28 sts and 12 sps.

Rnd 5: Slip st in next sc, ch 4, (dc in same st, ch 1) 4 times, ★ † sc in next ch-4 sp, sc in next Cluster (closing ch) and in next ch-4 sp, ch 1, skip next sc, (dc, ch 1) 5 times in next sc, 3 sc in next corner ch-3 sp, ch 1, skip next sc †, (dc, ch 1) 5 times in next sc; repeat from ★ 2 times **more**, then repeat from † to † once; join with slip st to first dc, finish off: 64 sts and 48 ch-1 sps.

Rnd 6: With **right** side facing, join Pink with sc in third ch-1 sp **after** any corner 3-sc group; ★ † sc in next dc and in next ch-1 sp, ch 4, work Cluster, ch 4, sc in next ch-1 sp, sc in next dc and in next ch-1 sp, ch 5, work Cluster, ch 5 †, sc in next ch-1 sp; repeat from ★ 2 times **more**, then repeat from † to † once, join with slip st to first sc: 32 sts and 16 sps.

Rnd 7: Slip st in next sc, ch 4, (dc in same st, ch 1) 4 times, ★ † sc in next ch-4 sp, sc in next Cluster and in next ch-4 sp, ch 1, skip next sc, (dc, ch 1) 5 times in next sc, 3 sc in next ch-5 sp, ch 1, (dc, ch 1) 5 times in next Cluster, 3 sc in next ch-5 sp, ch 1, skip next sc †, (dc, ch 1) 5 times in next sc; repeat from ★ 2 times **more**, then repeat from † to † once; join with slip st to first dc, finish off: 96 sts and 72 ch-1 sps.

Rnd 8: With **right** side facing, join Dk Pink with sc in ch-1 sp **after** center dc of any corner 5-dc group; 2 sc in same sp, ★ † ch 4, work Cluster, ch 4, [sc in next ch-1 sp, sc in next dc and in next ch-1 sp, ch 4, work Cluster, ch 4] across to within one ch-1 sp of center dc of next corner 5-dc group, 3 sc in next ch-1 sp, ch 5 †, 3 sc in next ch-1 sp; repeat from ★ 2 times **more**, then repeat from † to † once; join with slip st to first sc: 60 sts and 28 sps.

Rnd 9: Slip st in next sc, ch 4, (dc in same st, ch 1) 4 times, ★ † [sc in next ch-4 sp, sc in next Cluster and in next ch-4 sp, ch 1, skip next sc, (dc, ch 1) 5 times in next sc] across to next corner ch-5 sp, 3 sc in corner ch-5 sp, ch 1, skip next sc †, (dc, ch 1) 5 times in next sc; repeat from ★ 2 times **more**, then repeat from † to † once; join with slip st to first dc, finish off: 128 sts and 96 ch-1 sps.

Rnd 10: With **right** side facing, join Brown with sc in third ch-1 sp **after** any corner 3-sc group; ★ † sc in next dc and in next ch-1 sp, [ch 4, work Cluster, ch 4, sc in next ch-1 sp, sc in next dc and in next ch-1 sp] across to within 2 ch-1 sps of next corner 3-sc group, ch 5, work Cluster, ch 5 †, sc in next ch-1 sp; repeat from ★ 2 times **more**, then repeat from † to † once; join with slip st to first sc: 64 sts and 32 sps.

Rnd 11: Slip st in next sc, ch 4, (dc in same st, ch 1) 4 times, ★ † [sc in next ch-4 sp, sc in next Cluster and in next ch-4 sp, ch 1, skip next sc, (dc, ch 1) 5 times in next sc] across to next ch-5 sp, 3 sc in ch-5 sp, ch 1, (dc, ch 1) 5 times in next Cluster, 3 sc in next ch-5 sp, ch 1, skip next sc †, (dc, ch 1) 5 times in next sc; repeat from ★ 2 times **more**, then repeat from † to † once; join with slip st to first dc, finish off: 160 sts and 120 ch-1 sps.

Rnd 12: With **right** side facing, skip next 5 ch-1 sps **after** center dc of any corner 5-dc group and join Pink with sc in next ch-1 sp; ★ † sc in next dc and in next ch-1 sp, ch 4, work Cluster, [ch 4, sc in next ch-1 sp, sc in next dc and in next ch-1 sp, ch 4, work Cluster] across to within one ch-1 sp of center dc of next corner 5-dc group, ch 5, sc in next ch-1 sp, sc in next dc and in next ch-1 sp, ch 5, work Cluster, ch 4 †, sc in next ch-1 sp; repeat from ★ 2 times **more**, then repeat from † to † once; join with slip st to first sc: 80 sts and 40 sps.

Rnd 13: Slip st in next sc, ch 4, (dc in same st, ch 1) 4 times, sc in next sp, sc in next Cluster and in next sp, ch 1, skip next sc, ★ (dc, ch 1) 5 times in next sc, sc in next sp, sc in next Cluster and in next sp, ch 1, skip next sc; repeat from ★ around; join with slip st to first dc, finish off: 160 sts and 120 ch-1 sps.

Rnds 14-42: Repeat Rnds 8-13, 4 times; then repeat Rnds 8-12 once **more**: 240 sts and 120 sps.

Rnd 43: Slip st in next sc, ch 4, (dc in same st, ch 1) 4 times, ★ † sc in next ch-4 sp, sc in next Cluster and in next ch-4 sp, ch 1, skip next sc, [(dc, ch 1) 5 times in next sc, sc in next ch-4 sp, sc in next Cluster and in next sp, ch 1] across to next corner 3-sc group, skip next sc, (dc, ch 1) 7 times in next sc, sc in next ch-5 sp, sc in next Cluster and in next ch-4 sp, ch 1, skip next sc †, (dc, ch 1) 5 times in next sc; repeat from ★ 2 times **more**, then repeat from † to † once; join with slip st to first dc, finish off.

Crosses AND Blocks

Finished Size: 58½" (148.5 cm) square

EASY

SHOPPING LIST

Yarn (Medium Weight) MEDIUM 4
[3.5 ounces, 210 yards
(100 grams, 192 meters) per skein]:

- ☐ Blue - 4 skeins
- ☐ Green - 4 skeins
- ☐ Orange - 4 skeins

Crochet Hook

- ☐ Size I (5.5 mm)
  or size needed for gauge

GAUGE INFORMATION

In pattern,
2 repeats (14 dc and 4 chs) = 5" (12.75 cm)
Rnds 1-5 = 6" (15.25 cm)

Gauge Swatch: 6" (15.25 cm) square
Work same as Body through Rnd 5: 64 dc and 20 sps.

STITCH GUIDE

CROSS STITCH
(abbreviated Cross St)
(uses next 2 ch-1 sps)

Skip next ch-1 sp, dc in next ch-1 sp, working **around** dc just made, dc in skipped ch-1 sp.

INSTRUCTIONS

Body

With Blue, ch 5; join with slip st to form a ring.

Rnd 1 (Right side)**:** Ch 6 **(counts as first dc plus ch 3)**, (3 dc in ring, ch 3) 3 times, 2 dc in ring; join with slip st to first dc: 12 dc and 4 ch-3 sps.

Note: Loop a short piece of yarn around any stitch to mark Rnd 1 as **right** side.

Rnd 2: Slip st in next corner ch-3 sp; ch 3 **(counts as first dc, now and throughout)**, (dc, ch 3, 2 dc) in same sp, ch 1, skip next dc, 2 dc in next dc, ch 1, ★ (2 dc, ch 3, 2 dc) in next corner ch-3 sp, ch 1, skip next dc, 2 dc in next dc, ch 1; repeat from ★ 2 times **more**; join with slip st to first dc, finish off: 24 dc and 12 sps.

Rnd 3: With **right** side facing, join Green with dc in any corner ch-3 sp *(see Joining With Dc, page 31)*; (dc, ch 3, 2 dc) in same sp, dc in next 2 dc, ch 1, work Cross St, ch 1, dc in next 2 dc, ★ (2 dc, ch 3, 2 dc) in next corner ch-3 sp, dc in next 2 dc, ch 1, work Cross St, ch 1, dc in next 2 dc; repeat from ★ 2 times **more**; join with slip st to first dc: 40 dc and 12 sps.

Rnd 4: Ch 3, dc in next dc, ★ † (2 dc, ch 3, 2 dc) in next corner ch-3 sp, dc in next 4 dc, ch 1, work Cross St, ch 1 †, dc in next 4 dc; repeat from ★ 2 times **more**, then repeat † to † once, dc in last 2 dc; join with slip st to first dc, finish off: 56 dc and 12 sps.

Rnd 5: With **right** side facing, join Orange with dc in any corner ch-3 sp; (dc, ch 3, 2 dc) in same sp, ★ † ch 1, skip next dc, dc in next 5 dc, ch 1, work Cross St, ch 1, dc in next 5 dc, ch 1, skip next dc †, (2 dc, ch 3, 2 dc) in next corner ch-3 sp; repeat from ★ 2 times **more**, then repeat from † to † once; join with slip st to first dc: 64 dc and 20 sps.

Rnd 6: Ch 3, dc in next dc, ★ † ch 1, (2 dc, ch 3, 2 dc) in next corner ch-3 sp, ch 1, dc in next 2 dc, ch 1, dc in next 5 dc, ch 1, work Cross St, ch 1, dc in next 5 dc, ch 1 †, dc in next 2 dc; repeat from ★ 2 times **more**, then repeat from † to † once; join with slip st to first dc, finish off: 80 dc and 28 sps.

Rnd 7: With **right** side facing, join Green with dc in any corner ch-3 sp; (dc, ch 3, 2 dc) in same sp, ★ † dc in next 2 dc, ch 1, work Cross St, ch 1, (dc in next 5 dc, ch 1, work Cross St, ch 1) across to within 2 dc of next corner ch-3 sp, dc in next 2 dc †, (2 dc, ch 3, 2 dc) in corner ch-3 sp; repeat from ★ 2 times **more**, then repeat from † to † once; join with slip st to first dc, finish off: 96 dc and 28 sps.

Rnd 8: With **right** side facing, join Blue with dc in any corner ch-3 sp; (dc, ch 3, 2 dc) in same sp, ★ † dc in next 4 dc, ch 1, work Cross St, ch 1, (dc in next 5 dc, ch 1, work Cross St, ch 1) across to within 4 dc of next corner ch-3 sp, dc in next 4 dc †, (2 dc, ch 3, 2 dc) in corner ch-3 sp; repeat from ★ 2 times **more**, then repeat from † to † once; join with slip st to first dc, finish off: 112 dc and 28 sps.

Rnd 9: With **right** side facing, join Orange with dc in any corner ch-3 sp; (dc, ch 3, 2 dc) in same sp, ★ † ch 1, skip next dc, dc in next 5 dc, ch 1, (work Cross St, ch 1, dc in next 5 dc, ch 1) across to within one dc of next corner ch-3 sp, skip next dc †, (2 dc, ch 3, 2 dc) in corner ch-3 sp; repeat from ★ 2 times **more**, then repeat from † to † once; join with slip st to first dc, finish off: 120 dc and 36 sps.

Rnd 10: With **right** side facing, join Green with dc in any corner ch-3 sp; (dc, ch 3, 2 dc) in same sp, ★ † ch 1, dc in next 2 dc, ch 1, dc in next 5 dc, ch 1, (work Cross St, ch 1, dc in next 5 dc, ch 1) across to within 2 dc of next corner ch-3 sp, dc in next 2 dc, ch 1 †, (2 dc, ch 3, 2 dc) in corner ch-3 sp; repeat from ★ 2 times **more**, then repeat from † to † once; join with slip st to first dc; do **not** finish off: 136 dc and 44 sps.

Rnd 11: Ch 3, dc in next dc, ★ † (2 dc, ch 3, 2 dc) in next corner ch-3 sp, dc in next 2 dc, ch 1, work Cross St, ch 1, (dc in next 5 dc, ch 1, work Cross St, ch 1) across to within 2 dc of next corner ch-3 sp †, dc in next 2 dc; repeat from ★ 2 times **more**, then repeat from † to † once; join with slip st to first dc: 152 dc and 44 sps.

Rnd 12: Ch 3, dc in next 3 dc, ★ † (dc, ch 1, 2 dc, ch 3, 2 dc, ch 1, dc) in next corner ch-3 sp, dc in next 4 dc, ch 1, work Cross St, ch 1, (dc in next 5 dc, ch 1, work Cross St, ch 1) across to within 4 dc of next corner ch-3 sp †, dc in next 4 dc; repeat from ★ 2 times **more**, then repeat from † to † once; join with slip st to first dc, finish off: 176 dc and 52 sps.

Rnds 13-15: With Blue, repeat Rnds 10-12: 232 dc and 68 sps.

Rnds 16-18: With Orange, repeat Rnds 10-12: 288 dc and 84 sps.

Rnds 19 and 20: With Blue, repeat Rnds 10 and 11; at end of Rnd 20, finish off: 320 dc and 92 sps.

Rnd 21: With **right** side facing, join Green with dc in any corner ch-3 sp; (dc, ch 3, 2 dc, ch 1, dc) in same sp, ★ † dc in next 4 dc, ch 1, work Cross St, ch 1, (dc in next 5 dc, ch 1, work Cross St, ch 1) across to within 4 dc of next corner ch-3 sp, dc in next 4 dc †, (dc, ch 1, 2 dc, ch 3, 2 dc, ch 1, dc) in corner ch-3 sp; repeat from ★ 2 times **more**, then repeat from † to † once, dc in same sp as first dc, ch 1; join with slip st to first dc: 344 dc and 100 sps.

Rnd 22: Ch 3, dc in next dc, ch 1, ★ † (2 dc, ch 3, 2 dc) in next corner ch-3 sp, ch 1, dc in next 2 dc, ch 1, dc in next 5 dc, ch 1, (work Cross St, ch 1, dc in next 5 dc, ch 1) across to within 2 dc of next corner ch-3 sp †, dc in next 2 dc, ch 1; repeat from ★ 2 times **more**, then repeat from † to † once; join with slip st to first dc, finish off: 360 dc and 108 sps.

Rnd 23: With **right** side facing, join Orange with dc in any corner ch-3 sp; (dc, ch 3, 2 dc) in same sp, ★ † dc in next 2 dc, ch 1, work Cross St, ch 1, (dc in next 5 dc, ch 1, work Cross St, ch 1) across to within 2 dc of next corner ch-3 sp, dc in next 2 dc †, (2 dc, ch 3, 2 dc) in corner ch-3 sp; repeat from ★ 2 times **more**, then repeat from † to † once; join with slip st to first dc: 376 dc and 108 sps.

Rnd 24: Ch 3, dc in next dc, ★ † (dc, ch 1, 2 dc, ch 3, 2 dc, ch 1, dc) in next corner ch-3 sp, dc in next 4 dc, ch 1, work Cross St, ch 1, (dc in next 5 dc, ch 1, work Cross St, ch 1) across to within 4 dc of next corner ch-3 sp †, dc in next 4 dc; repeat from ★ 2 times **more**, then repeat from † to † once, dc in last 2 dc; join with slip st to first dc, finish off: 400 dc and 116 sps.

Rnd 25: With **right** side facing, join Green with dc in any corner ch-3 sp; (dc, ch 3, 2 dc) in same sp, ★ † ch 1, dc in next 2 dc, ch 1, dc in next 5 dc, ch 1, (work Cross St, ch 1, dc in next 5 dc, ch 1) across to within 2 dc of next corner ch-3 sp, dc in next 2 dc, ch 1 †, (2 dc, ch 3, 2 dc) in corner ch-3 sp; repeat from ★ 2 times **more**, then repeat from † to † once; join with slip st to first dc; finish off: 416 dc and 124 sps.

Rnd 26: With **right** side facing, join Blue with dc in any corner ch-3 sp; (dc, ch 3, 2 dc) in same sp, ★ † dc in next 2 dc, ch 1, work Cross St, ch 1, (dc in next 5 dc, ch 1, work Cross St, ch 1) across to within 2 dc of next corner ch-3 sp, dc in next 2 dc †, (2 dc, ch 3, 2 dc) in corner ch-3 sp; repeat from ★ 2 times **more**, then repeat from † to † once; join with slip st to first dc, finish off: 432 dc and 124 sps.

Rnd 27: With **right** side facing, join Orange with dc in any corner ch-3 sp; (dc, ch 3, 2 dc) in same sp, ★ † dc in next 4 dc, ch 1, work Cross St, ch 1, (dc in next 5 dc, ch 1, work Cross St, ch 1) across to within 4 dc of next corner ch-3 sp, dc in next 4 dc †, (2 dc, ch 3, 2 dc) in corner ch-3 sp; repeat from ★ 2 times **more**, then repeat from † to † once; join with slip st to first dc, finish off: 448 dc and 124 sps.

Rnd 28: With **right** side facing, join Green with dc in any corner ch-3 sp; (dc, ch 3, 2 dc) in same sp, ★ † ch 1, skip next dc, dc in next 5 dc, ch 1, (work Cross St, ch 1, dc in next 5 dc, ch 1) across to within one dc of next corner ch-3 sp, skip next dc †, (2 dc, ch 3, 2 dc) in corner ch-3 sp; repeat from ★ 2 times **more**, then repeat from † to † once; join with slip st to first dc: 456 dc and 132 sps.

Rnd 29: Slip st in next dc and in next corner ch-3 sp, ch 3, (dc, ch 3, 2 dc) in same sp, ★ † ch 1, dc in next 2 dc, ch 1, dc in next 5 dc, ch 1, (work Cross St, ch 1, dc in next 5 dc, ch 1) across to within 2 dc of next corner ch-3 sp, dc in next 2 sts, ch 1 †, (2 dc, ch 3, 2 dc) in corner ch-3 sp; repeat from ★ 2 times **more**, then repeat from † to † once; join with slip st to first dc: 472 dc and 140 sps.

Rnd 30: Ch 3, dc in next dc, ★ † (2 dc, ch 3, 2 dc) in next corner ch-3 sp, dc in next 2 dc, ch 1, work Cross St, ch 1, (dc in next 5 dc, ch 1, work Cross St, ch 1) across to within 2 dc of next corner ch-3 sp †, dc in next 2 dc; repeat from ★ 2 times **more**, then repeat from † to † once; join with slip st to first dc; finish off: 488 dc and 140 sps.

Rnd 31: With **right** side facing, join Blue with dc in any corner ch-3 sp; (dc, ch 3, 2 dc) in same sp, ★ † dc in next 4 dc, ch 1, work Cross St, ch 1, (dc in next 5 dc, ch 1, work Cross St, ch 1) across to within 4 dc of next corner ch-3 sp, dc in next 4 dc †, (2 dc, ch 3, 2 dc) in corner ch-3 sp; repeat from ★ 2 times **more**, then repeat from † to † once; join with slip st to first dc: 504 dc and 140 sps.

Rnd 32: Slip st in next dc and in next corner ch-3 sp, ch 3, (dc, ch 3, 2 dc) in same sp, ★ † ch 1, skip next dc, dc in next 5 dc, ch 1, (work Cross St, ch 1, dc in next 5 dc, ch 1) across to within one dc of next corner ch-3 sp, skip next dc †, (2 dc, ch 3, 2 dc) in corner ch-3 sp; repeat from ★ 2 times **more**, then repeat from † to † once; join with slip st to first dc: 512 dc and 148 sps.

Rnd 33: Ch 3, dc in next dc, ch 1, ★ † (2 dc, ch 3, 2 dc) in next corner ch-3 sp, ch 1, dc in next 2 dc, ch 1, dc in next 5 dc, ch 1, (work Cross St, ch 1, dc in next 5 dc, ch 1) across to within 2 dc of next corner ch-3 sp †, dc in next 2 dc, ch 1; repeat from ★ 2 times **more**, then repeat from † to † once; join with slip st to first dc, finish off: 528 dc and 156 sps.

Rnd 34: With **right** side facing, join Orange with dc in any corner ch-3 sp; (dc, ch 3, 2 dc) in same sp, ★ † dc in next 2 dc, ch 1, work Cross St, ch 1, (dc in next 5 dc, ch 1, work Cross St, ch 1) across to within 2 dc of next corner ch-3 sp, dc in next 2 dc †, (2 dc, ch 3, 2 dc) in corner ch-3 sp; repeat from ★ 2 times **more**, then repeat from † to † once; join with slip st to first dc: 544 dc and 156 sps.

Rnd 35: Ch 3, dc in next dc, (2 dc, ch 3, 2 dc) in next corner ch-3 sp, dc in next 4 dc, ch 1, work Cross St, ch 1, ★ (dc in next 5 dc, ch 1, work Cross St, ch 1) across to within 4 dc of next corner ch-3 sp, dc in next 4 dc, (2 dc, ch 3, 2 dc) in corner ch-3 sp, dc in next 4 dc, ch 1, work Cross St, ch 1; repeat from ★ 2 times **more**, (dc in next 5 dc, ch 1, work Cross St, ch 1) across to last 2 dc, dc in last 2 dc; join with slip st to first dc: 560 dc and 156 sps.

Rnd 36: Ch 3, dc in next 2 dc, ch 1, skip next dc, (2 dc, ch 3, 2 dc) in next corner ch-3 sp, ch 1, ★ skip next dc, dc in next 5 dc, ch 1, (work Cross St, ch 1, dc in next 5 dc, ch 1) across to within one dc of next corner ch-3 sp, skip next dc, (2 dc, ch 3, 2 dc) in next corner ch-3 sp, ch 1; repeat from ★ 2 times **more**, skip next dc, (dc in next 5 dc, ch 1, work Cross St, ch 1) across to last 2 dc, dc in last 2 dc; join with slip st to first dc, finish off: 568 dc and 164 sps.

Rnds 37 and 38: With Blue, repeat Rnds 10 and 11; at end of Rnd 38, finish off: 600 dc and 172 sps.

Rnds 39 and 40: With Green, repeat Rnds 31 and 32; at end of Rnd 40, finish off: 624 dc and 180 sps:

Rnds 41 and 42: With Orange, repeat Rnds 10 and 11: 656 dc and 188 sps.

Finish off.

Sand AND Sky

Shown on page 29.

Finished Size: 51" (129.5 cm) square

EASY

SHOPPING LIST

Yarn (Medium Weight) MEDIUM 4

[7 ounces, 370 yards
(198 grams, 338 meters) per skein]:

☐ Tan - 4 skeins

[5 ounces, 230 yards
(141 grams, 211 meters) per skein]:

☐ Variegated - 2 skeins

Crochet Hook

☐ Size K (6.5 mm)
or size needed for gauge

GAUGE INFORMATION

In pattern,
(sc, ch 1, 7 tr, ch 1) = 3½" (9 cm);
Rnds 1 and 2 = 4½" (11.5 cm)

Gauge Swatch: 4½" (11.5 cm) square

Work same as Body through Rnd 2:
32 sts and 8 ch-1 sps.

STITCH GUIDE

TREBLE CROCHET
(abbreviated tr)

YO twice, insert hook in st or sp indicated, YO and pull up a loop (4 loops on hook), (YO and draw through 2 loops on hook) 3 times.

INSTRUCTIONS

Body

With Variegated, ch 5; join with slip st to form a ring.

Rnd 1 (Right side)**:** Ch 5 **(counts as first tr plus ch 1, now and throughout)**, tr in ring, ch 2, ★ (tr, ch 1, tr) in ring, ch 2; repeat from ★ 2 times **more**; join with slip st to first tr, finish off: 8 tr and 8 sps.

Note: Loop a short piece of yarn around any stitch to mark Rnd 1 as **right** side.

Rnd 2: With **right** side facing, join Tan with sc in any ch-1 sp ***(see Joining With Sc, page 31)***; ch 1, 7 tr in next ch-2 sp, ch 1, ★ sc in next ch-1 sp, ch 1, 7 tr in next ch-2 sp, ch 1; repeat from ★ 2 times **more**; join with slip st to first sc, finish off: 32 sts and 8 ch-1 sps.

Rnd 3: With **right** side facing, join Variegated with slip st in any sc; ch 5, (tr, ch 4, tr, ch 1, tr) in same st, ★ † ch 3, skip next 3 tr, sc in next tr, ch 3, skip next 3 tr †, (tr, ch 1, tr, ch 4, tr, ch 1, tr) in next sc; repeat from ★ 2 times **more**, then repeat from † to † once; join with slip st to first tr, finish off: 20 sts and 20 sps.

Rnd 4: With **right** side facing, join Tan with sc in any corner ch-4 sp; ★ † ch 1, 7 tr in next ch-1 sp, ch 1, skip next ch-3 sp, sc in next sc, ch 1, skip next ch-3 sp, 7 tr in next ch-1 sp, ch 1 †, sc in next corner ch-4 sp; repeat from ★ 2 times **more**, then repeat from † to † once; join with slip st to first sc, finish off: 64 sts and 16 ch-1 sps.

Rnd 5: With **right** side facing, join Variegated with slip st in any corner sc; ch 5, (tr, ch 4, tr, ch 1, tr) in same st, ★ † ch 3, skip next 3 tr, sc in next tr, ch 3, skip next 3 tr, (tr, ch 1, tr) in next sc, ch 3, skip next 3 tr, sc in next tr, ch 3, skip next 3 tr †, (tr, ch 1, tr, ch 4, tr, ch 1, tr) in next sc; repeat from ★ 2 times **more**, then repeat from † to † once; join with slip st to first tr, finish off: 32 sts and 32 sps.

Rnd 6: With **right** side facing, join Tan with sc in any corner ch-4 sp; ★ † ch 1, 7 tr in next ch-1 sp, ch 1, [skip next ch-3 sp, sc in next sc, ch 1, skip next ch-3 sp, 7 tr in next ch-1 sp, ch 1] across to next corner ch-4 sp †, sc in corner ch-4 sp; repeat from ★ 2 times **more**, then repeat from † to † once; join with slip st to first sc, finish off: 96 sts and 24 ch-1 sps.

Rnd 7: With **right** side facing, join Variegated with slip st in any corner sc; ch 5, (tr, ch 4, tr, ch 1, tr) in same st, ★ † ch 3, skip next 3 tr, sc in next tr, ch 3, skip next 3 tr, [(tr, ch 1, tr) in next sc, ch 3, skip next 3 tr, sc in next tr, ch 3, skip next 3 tr] across to next corner sc †, (tr, ch 1, tr, ch 4, tr, ch 1, tr) in corner sc; repeat from ★ 2 times **more**, then repeat from † to † once; join with slip st to first tr, finish off: 44 sts and 44 sps.

Rnds 8-28: Repeat Rnds 6 and 7, 10 times; then repeat Rnd 6 once **more**: 448 sts and 112 ch-1 sps.

General Instructions

ABBREVIATIONS

ch(s)	chain(s)
cm	centimeters
dc	double crochet(s)
dtr	double treble crochet(s)
mm	millimeters
Rnd(s)	Round(s)
sc	single crochet(s)
sp(s)	space(s)
st(s)	stitch(es)
tr	treble crochet(s)
YO	yarn over

SYMBOLS & TERMS

★ — work instructions following ★ as many **more** times as indicated in addition to the first time.

† to † — work all instructions from first † to second † **as many** times as specified.

( ) or **[ ]** — work enclosed instructions **as many** times as specified by the number immediately following **or** work all enclosed instructions in the stitch or space indicated **or** contains explanatory remarks.

colon (:) — the number(s) given after a colon at the end of a row or round denote(s) the number of stitches or spaces you should have on that row or round.

CROCHET TERMINOLOGY		
UNITED STATES		INTERNATIONAL
slip stitch (slip st)	=	single crochet (sc)
single crochet (sc)	=	double crochet (dc)
half double crochet (hdc)	=	half treble crochet (htr)
double crochet (dc)	=	treble crochet (tr)
treble crochet (tr)	=	double treble crochet (dtr)
double treble crochet (dtr)	=	triple treble crochet (ttr)
triple treble crochet (tr tr)	=	quadruple treble crochet (qtr)
skip	=	miss

BEGINNER	Projects for first-time crocheters using basic stitches. Minimal shaping.
EASY	Projects using yarn with basic stitches, repetitive stitch patterns, simple color changes, and simple shaping and finishing.
INTERMEDIATE	Projects using a variety of techniques, such as basic lace patterns or color patterns, mid-level shaping and finishing.
EXPERIENCED	Projects with intricate stitch patterns, techniques and dimension, such as non-repeating patterns, multi-color techniques, fine threads, small hooks, detailed shaping and refined finishing.

GAUGE

Exact gauge is **essential** for proper size. Before beginning your Afghan, make the sample swatch given in the individual instructions in the yarn and hook specified. After completing the swatch, measure it, counting your stitches and rounds or rows carefully. If your swatch is larger or smaller than specified, **make another, changing hook size to get the correct gauge**. Keep trying until you find the size hook that will give you the specified gauge.

JOINING WITH DC

When instructed to join with dc, begin with a slip knot on the hook. YO, holding loop on the hook, insert the hook in the stitch or space indicated, YO and pull up a loop (3 loops on hook), (YO and draw through 2 loops on hook) twice.

WORKING AROUND A STITCH

Work in stitch or space indicated, inserting hook in direction of arrow *(Fig. 1)*.

Fig. 1

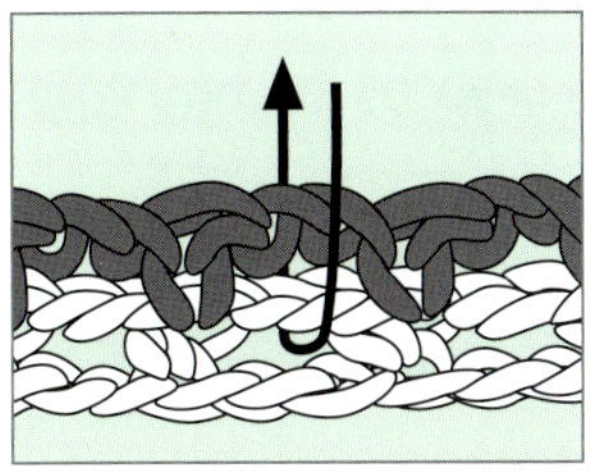

JOINING WITH SC

When instructed to join with sc, begin with a slip knot on the hook. Insert the hook in the stitch or space indicated, YO and pull up a loop, YO and draw through both loops on the hook.

Yarn Weight Symbol & Names	LACE 0	SUPER FINE 1	FINE 2	LIGHT 3	MEDIUM 4	BULKY 5	SUPER BULKY 6	JUMBO 7
Type of Yarns in Category	Fingering, size 10 crochet thread	Sock, Fingering, Baby	Sport, Baby	DK, Light Worsted	Worsted, Afghan, Aran	Chunky, Craft, Rug	Super Bulky, Roving	Jumbo, Roving
Crochet Gauge* Ranges in Single Crochet to 4" (10 cm)	32-42 sts**	21-32 sts	16-20 sts	12-17 sts	11-14 sts	8-11 sts	6-9 sts	5 sts and fewer
Advised Hook Size Range	Steel*** 6 to 8, Regular hook B-1	B-1 to E-4	E-4 to 7	7 to I-9	I-9 to K-10½	K-10½ to M/N-13	M/N-13 to Q	Q and larger

*GUIDELINES ONLY: The chart above reflects the most commonly used gauges and hook sizes for specific yarn categories.

** Lace weight yarns are usually crocheted with larger hooks to create lacy openwork patterns. Accordingly, a gauge range is difficult to determine. Always follow the gauge stated in your pattern.

*** Steel crochet hooks are sized differently from regular hooks–the higher the number, the smaller the hook, which is the reverse of regular hook sizing.

CROCHET HOOKS																	
U.S.	B-1	C-2	D-3	E-4	F-5	G-6	7	H-8	I-9	J-10	K-10½	L-11	M/N-13	N/P-15	P/Q	Q	S
Metric - mm	2.25	2.75	3.25	3.5	3.75	4	4.5	5	5.5	6	6.5	8	9	10	15	16	19

Yarn Information

Each Afghan in this book was made using Medium Weight yarn. It is best to refer to the yardage/meters when determining how many balls or skeins to purchase. Remember, to achieve the finished size, it is the GAUGE/TENSION that is important, not the brand of yarn.

For your convenience, listed below are the specific yarns used to create our photography models. Because yarn manufacturers make frequent changes in their product lines, you may sometimes find it necessary to use a substitute yarn or to search for the discontinued product at alternate suppliers (locally or online).

LOG CABIN

Caron® One Pound™

Purple - #10547 Deep Violet

Lilac - #10577 Lilac

Rose - #10535 Country Rose

Pink - #10513 Soft Pink

EARTHY SHADOWS

Patons® Décor™

Tan - #87631 Taupe

Variegated - #87698 Tapestry Variegated

JEWELS

Red Heart® Soft®

Wine - #4608 Wine

Gold - #9114 Honey

Blue - #9820 Mid Blue

Green - #9621 True Green

PATCHWORK

Lion Brand® Heartland®

Tan - #398 Arcadia Tweed

Green - #373 Everglades Tweed

PATRIOTIC LACE

Caron® Simply Soft®

Off White - #9702 Off White

Blue - #9710 Country Blue

Red - #9730 Autumn Red

PINK PASSION

Lion Brand® Vanna's Choice®

Pink - #101 Pink

Dk Pink - #112 Raspberry

Brown - #124 Toffee

CROSSES AND BLOCKS

Patons® Classic Wool Worsted™

Blue - #77132 Royal Blue

Green - #77708 Emerald

Orange - #77605 Pumpkin

SAND AND SKY

Red Heart® With Love®

Tan - #1308 Tan

Variegated - #1938 Beachy

We have made every effort to ensure that these instructions are accurate and complete. We cannot, however, be responsible for human error, typographical mistakes, or variations in individual work.

Production Team: Writer/Instructional Editor - Sarah J. Green; Editorial Writer - Susan Frantz Wiles; Senior Graphic Artist - Lora Puls; Graphic Artist - Victoria Temple; Photo Stylist - Lori Wenger; and Photographer - Mark Mathews.